SMALL TALK WITH MYSELF

SMALL TALK WITH MYSELF
Reflections on Pandemic Single Life

L.B. Lewis

E-Book Kindle ISBN: 978-0-9978928-6-4
Paperback ISBN: 978-0-9978928-9-5

ISBN Genres: Wit and Humor, Memoir, Non-fiction

Table of Contents

Introduction

While coloring a frog in kindergarten, Sr. Justin laid a hearty pat on my butt just when I was reaching across the table for another crayon. She told me frogs were green. I defended my purple-spotted frog with "he's sick" and sat down.

Doing things differently has always come naturally to me. When someone asked me how I was adjusting to the new normal at the pandemic's start, I was completely caught off guard. Using the word normal was new to me, and adding new into the mix, was definitely not normal.

This book unofficially started around my birthday in late March 2020. It was shortly after shelter-in-place started in the San Francisco Bay Area. I kept writing down little accounts of my lockdown life for posterity and processing, and well, really to fight off boredom. Days seemed nameless, and at times there were way too many Mondays in a row. The year 2020 seemed to be at least one dog year for some of us, maybe more.

What follows here is a collection of personal reflections about how I spent the pandemic from March 2020 to June 2021 as a single woman living in Oakland, California. My journey through the pandemic was spent in a rent-controlled studio, mainly going to the laundromat and supermarket, writing, and practicing the art of self-entertainment, which included making small talk with myself, sometimes making videos, attempting a podcast, and attending over 400 virtual events. Many memories, including quite a few from 9/11, came up along the way while writing this. In hindsight, my feelings of nostalgia helped me write this book. And, looking forward, what I know I'll remember about the pandemic is how much time I had.

When I got the vaccine in May 2021, I felt like I had a pandemic hangover and, at the same time, more optimistic about the future. Unfortunately, the pandemic is not over at the time of publishing, and our shared recovery narrative continues slowly to the unknown.

My heartfelt thanks to all those who supported this work and me during the pandemic. I'm grateful for life's surprises and the stories that come with them.

1 Small Talk with Myself

I love small talk. I love everything about it. But most people don't like small talk. That's according to a poll I took on Twitter during the pandemic.

The thing is, if you hate small talk enough to take a poll, you must like polls. And, can't polls be a type of small talk?

But, for me, small talk has never been about words. Or polls. Sure, the words matter. So does the timing. But there's something more...

I can say with confidence that I am an expert in keeping myself entertained. I'm also pretty good at doing it for free.

When my childhood imaginary friends appeared, this was the start of something big. You probably had them, too. Mine liked everything I did and were always up for small talk. I don't know where I met them or how we got to be friends, but we really did have a lot of fun.

Once, we had this amazing tea party where I prepared everything and served my friends. Then, I sat down, and we all laughed together and drank our tea. I'm not even sure I knew what tea was at that age growing up in Cleveland, but I do remember having the best time. Then, they disappeared. They probably got better jobs somewhere or got married to billionaires to hire someone to post on social media all day.

Truth be told, I'm not upset my imaginary friends ghosted me. I wasn't expecting them to show up during the pandemic anyway. I went back to a habit I started on 9/11. I remember my phone stopped working on my way to class at Georgetown. Then I found out it was working again when I texted myself. On slow days, and there were a lot during the pandemic, my texts served both a functional and creative purpose. And, once and a while, I even would write myself a pretend horoscope promising brighter days, unexpected income, and a friend from the past returning. A running text diary of messages from me to me was fun.

But, officially though, my pandemic small talk with myself began on my birthday at the end of March 2020, roughly two weeks after the lockdown started in the San Francisco Bay Area. My neighborhood had become eerily quiet with no traffic or the screechy BART noise.

To leave my apartment required preparation, both mentally and physically, by masking up and taking hand sanitizer. It all felt like going on a big trip. And, on this day, that trip was to France. I wanted to get a pain au chocolat for my birthday breakfast at a small French bakery in Berkeley. I was feeling nostalgic about my summers working in Paris. Back then, I'd like to go to as many different boulangeries as I could to see the different pastries, make price comparisons, and do a taste test of almond croissants.

When I finally got to the bakery in Berkeley, it was closed. "Where can I go to get a pain au chocolat?" I asked out loud to no one. It was logical to take out my phone to look. But I didn't want to. I thought for a moment and then answered my question for myself and walked to another bakery.

Before the pandemic, my Midwestern friendliness showed up regularly in these types of interactions and opportunities for small talk. The day shelter-in-place was announced, I was temping and didn't understand what was going on until the executive director said, "You need to go home and stay there." Then, that's what I did for all of 2020 and most of 2021.

Like many people experiencing this new normal, I had to pivot and find another job. Or jobs. For the record, I would spend most of my time in 2020 applying for jobs. Years earlier, at a communications workshop for women in San Francisco, I had learned for maximum presentation value, a computer should always be higher than your head for the most flattering angle, and you should wear a V-neck because they tend to look good on every body type.

So, I stacked old shoe boxes on my kitchen table and wore my only V-neck sweater as much as possible for interviews. As shelter-in-place continued for months, I found myself talking more with myself, on and off camera. A big part of my identity was coming from seeing myself in a box on my computer screen. Then, I evolved to actively practicing being natural while "thinking out of the box" for interviews in a box, when I practiced Zoom calls by myself. I always started with small talk.

In June, a blog post I wrote about ageism was

selected as one of Hacker Noon's "Top 25 of 2020." I was elated and really hoped that this would translate into a job. In reality, I didn't know if my long job search during the pandemic and time spent waiting was because of my age or how my V-neck sweater looked in a box.

Things started to change when I started taking virtual improv classes at the beginning of 2021. My small talk skills got both a boost and a bigger audience. But I'll always remember how much time I had during the pandemic to build a better relationship with myself. I gained a new understanding and appreciation for those that choose to marry themselves. I felt like, I too, had more of a committed relationship with my party of one, always ready to talk and listen.

2 Pistachio Palace

Most people don't know this but the only thing that is under control in a rent-controlled apartment is the rent. Everything else...well, that is up to interpretation.

In October 2014, I showed up at an open house for a rent-controlled interior studio in Oakland. I had returned from working in Paris and was exhausted from trying to find something safe and that I could afford in the San Francisco Bay Area.

The place's paint job as well as its history were patchy, to say the least. I was told that the ground floor, which was retail space, was built around 1920. Then, so the legend goes, the second story was built a year later. Another year later, the final story was added.

The outside of the building was painted not one but two tones of pistachio green. The lighter shade was for the apartments; darker green for street retail. Later, when I lived there for some time, I concluded the darker green was just a paint-over for graffiti that happened once and awhile.

People that visited me were too polite to mention the apartment's major defect. But everyone noticed right away. You see, the whole apartment was off a few degrees to the left. That's not a metaphor. If you followed the slant out the window, you would see the floor's distorted angle relative to the skylights of the hair salon. You would also notice that the original hardwood flooring had a few "bumps" throughout the main room. I never asked what happened there.

This 1920's studio had almost all of its original fixtures. I was told it was the last one like it left in the building. The built-in, five-drawer dresser with the antique mirror, crystal knobs, and two-sided shelving added a touch of faded elegance to the main room. The former Murphy bed was transformed into a nook with glass doors. The kitchen had two obsolete, built-in wood cutting boards (gross) that faced modern cabinetry, a gas stove, and a twenty-year-old refrigerator that leaked sometimes. Although updated from the 1920s, the bathroom kept some of its charm, renovated with classic, white hexagon tiles and a claw foot tub.

Before shelter-in-place started in March 2020, there was an all-night party at one of the retail spaces below. Whatever was happening down there, the noise from parties continued intermittently after we were locked down, even though the county prohibited gatherings. Maybe it was the hair salon, marketing a haircut plus party pandemic promo.

Throughout the following six months, there'd be loud music ranging from electronic dance music to classical at all times of the day, but not every day. And then it all stopped around October of 2020. But the free WiFi that started with the lockdown continued.

There was a sort of changing of the guard with the new tenets of 2020. I heard through my walls neighbors, too, having parties during the lockdown in their apartments. One day, I was in my underwear on my bed with the blinds up and heard, "And this is our interior view," which was really me. I closed my blinds more often from then on.

Another time during the pandemic, I heard about a "beer club" that was meeting on the roof. The roof was now home to many more satellite dishes than when I moved in, which would make the "beer club" appealing to a select group of people that liked radiation and risk. When I went up to the roof one day in August to take a skyline photo for social media, there were, sure enough, many old beer cans around.

I think the same people behind the "beer club" were the ones that got a rusty rowing machine and some 80's looking tan and turquoise lawn furniture for the new hangout space in the back near the garages. I only saw people hanging out once there, then all that stuff got pushed to a corner.

The tenant rumored to have been living the longest in Pistachio Palace was my upstairs' neighbor. Pre-pandemic, he had a leak in his bathroom that filled my bathroom light with gray water. The building's seemingly unfixable water problems also had many kitchen sinks filling up with six inches of black water a few years ago.

I forgot to tell you about my studio's closet that was so large, it could have been another bedroom. During a particularly stressful time, I slept there since it was quiet and totally dark. I also mediated there a few times. It was a type of bunker, a quiet and dark space that felt safer than the main room. But not like the billionaire bunkers you read about that high-profile Silicon Valley people whisk their families away to eat meal-ready packs when the aliens are about to land or there's a nuclear disaster. For the record, I never took food in my closet, not even during the pandemic.

It was a relief when five neighbors moved out at the beginning of 2021. Then it was disorientating when a microbrewery so big I called it a macrobrewery moved in, setting up ten picnic tables in the back where the rowing machine used to be.

Soon after, I found a syringe near the front of the building, and I had another leak in my bathroom ceiling. When I told my landlord, they wanted to wait a week to fix it. From that phone call, I learned the neighbor upstairs was dying and had caregivers coming in and out. And, the homeless man that had defecated on our building weeks earlier came back and slept in the same brown spot he had previously created.

By mid-2021, my neighbor had passed away. A few weeks later, I, too, had moved on and out with no regrets.

3 Cat Sharing Economy

I'm proud to support the cat sharing economy. That's only if cats support it, too.

It's not that I never wanted a pet. It's just that I never got around to owning one. Yet.

Close to the Pistachio Palace, a pet store regularly had cats for adoption in the window. I frequently visited to say hello to the newcomers. Those cats never lasted long, leaving for somewhere, hopefully, better than a metal cage.

There were also several housecats in my neighborhood that would be on cat patrol at any given time. Some would come to say hello to passersby, like Ophelia, who was known to dart out of her yard to greet neighbors, like myself, who liked to stop and say hello.

Growing up in the '80s, I was fine sharing Garfield with millions. I never thought I would own a Garfield or Odie, so sharing was just fine by me. And while our family had a dog, he wasn't particularly friendly towards me, or for that matter, most people. I would try to buy his affection with treats and toys, which worked temporarily. As much as I wanted to dress him up and take naps with him, that never happened.

One of the best roommates and writing partners I ever had was an orange tabby named Caddy, who was my roommate's cat in Washington, D.C. He was large, like Garfield, and very vocal. This roommate was getting a divorce and, as I moved in, her ex-husband moved out. Caddy went through a phase and kept peeing on his owner's things, but not on my things. One day, he escaped when the back door was left open but came back when someone found him hiding in their garage. The day I moved the last box out of my room, he jetted in and did a lap around the empty room looking at me, then darted out.

In Madrid, I found a cat vortex. It was really a creek close to the school where I worked as an English auxiliary. We're not talking about a few cats; we're talking about twenty feral cats hanging out at any given time. White, black, orange, or striped, they were beautifully wild and hungry when I approached one day with open cans of food. I got the idea because my friend used to feed stray cats in the San Francisco Bay Area. I went with her once to feed them and thought it was a nice idea. But once by myself was enough for me. I was nervous about what they would do after finishing the food and didn't stick around to find out.

At one point during the pandemic, the giant house that looked like it belonged in a luxury magazine with the gray exterior and red-trimmed windows displayed a small chalkboard near the stone steps that read, "Please, Don't Pet the Cat."

Their fluffy orange cat was frequently perched to the right of the sign. That cat and I went way back.

That cat used to cross the street and come to say hello to me before the pandemic. I had known this orange cat to be extremely social for many years and, now, it, too, looked bored and lonely, just like me. I counted there were three signs total around the lawn asking people not to touch the cat.

The more I thought about the signs, the less I understood what was going on. The luxury house continued to have a free box near the stop sign with no warning about possibly being exposed to coronavirus from surface contact of that stuff. There were no other signs in the neighborhood like those, and the neighborhood cats were still out and about on cat patrol.

After reading online, it occurred to me that a person who would pet the cat could either give the cat coronavirus or the cat could give them coronavirus. I remember looking for more information online and getting lost by looking at daily statistics of the number of cases and deaths in Alameda County.

When I was asked to write an article about coronavirus, I continued to find many conflicting sources about the disease and how you could get it. It was a time of great confusion and anxiety with a deluge of information. My article never was published. At the end of June 2020, I did a week-long digital detox and put myself on a disciplined schedule to limit my time on social media, which helped me focus more on job searching and writing.

The signs asking people not to pet the cat stayed up at that house for many months in 2020. The free box gradually expanded to a free area, taking up one full tree lawn. There was everything from water bottles to furniture. A few times, I saw boxes of clothes. All of it vanished regularly.

The cat still stayed close to the house, and I only once saw it migrating to the other side of the street. Then, one day the signs disappeared, and only the small chalkboard remained. Soon after, the free area, chalkboard, and other things were replaced with a "For Rent" sign in the window.

4 The Laundromat Club

"You want to buy some deodorant?" asked the maskless man, two feet from my face while showing me a Secret deodorant. I shook my head rapidly and slammed down the washer lid. He said he had razor blades, too, after I turned away. I took a walk during the 29-minute wash cycle, and he was gone by the time I got back.

The laundromat near the Pistachio Palace was always unpredictable. This laundromat club was a revolving door of the circle of life. I never saw the same person twice except the owners and one owner's son. And, I never saw the exhaust fan without gray dust globs.

When I first moved into the neighborhood, the laundromat had a dog. The dog was the best part of the laundromat, even if he did smell. He lived with his owner, who was the manager in the back apartment that was attached to the laundromat. The dog was out near the washers and dryers more than the manager. He would happily greet people and jump in their lap if they were sitting. But the dog always smelled. Really it was ironic because, in a place where people went to wash their clothes, no one washed the poor smelly dog.

I know about being called smelly. I got evicted once in my life at the ripe age of 34. And the reason I got evicted was that I was told I smell first and that I worked from home second. The owner told me directly that my body odor was so strong that I made the room I rented smell, too. She asked that I clean the room so that she could rent it out again to someone that didn't smell. She also said that I was bringing duck poop into the house when I walked where ducks had been. And, she couldn't be around duck poop. After one month, I was gone.

A few years back, the laundromat manager and the smelly dog left. Someone said they had gotten evicted. A father and son came to manage the laundromat. One day, the father offered me some pastries and told me I could stay as long as I wanted to use the free WiFi. Another time, the 20-something-year-old son climbed up on the wall that separated the washers and looked down at us doing our laundry. It appeared it was his laundry day, too, just getting by with what very little he had left.

During the pandemic, I was very hesitant to go to any laundromat. I had been doing most of my laundry by hand in my tub from March to May 2020, and to my surprise, I enjoyed it. I felt like a pioneer woman and thought back to how I wish I had my grandmother's wringer. When I finally did return to the laundromat club, there was never any sign or anyone to enforce using masks at the laundromat during the pandemic. There'd be no one there on good days, and I could sit and read or use the WiFi. The number of customers seemed to decrease substantially during 2020, even on the weekends.

It blew my mind during the change shortage, where so many other businesses would say they couldn't give out the proper change; the laundromat consistently had a steady supply of quarters. For the record, there wasn't a time I went in 2020 that the change machine at the laundromat wasn't in operation.

Don't forget that the laundry library continued to be in operation there, too. Same as it ever was. The books were mostly children's books that were retired from local libraries. About two years ago, a boy around three was hovering in front of the book stand. His mom was on her cellphone loading clothes into a machine. He turned to me with a book. I started making some small talk with him. Then he gave me the book and crawled in my lap, just like the dog used to do. But this was long after the dog had left. I read him the story, and then his mom said they had to go. Of course, I never saw them again.

The worst day at the laundromat was a tie between when I saw a man washing his face with hand sanitizer and when my grocery cart that doubled as a laundry cart got stolen. After my cart got stolen, I promptly stopped being part of that laundromat club, preferring the larger one a few blocks further from the Pistachio Palace, now using my large suitcase.

5 Coffee Break

I love coffee. But it wasn't always this way. Here's why: most people don't know this, but in high school, I was in a training video for a large donut chain. My donut boss said I did a great job at the drive-through and that I spoke clearly. So that's how that happened, but I never saw the video they filmed, even though I looked for it once in and a while online.

I worked at that donut shop partly because my swim coach liked those donuts and partly because it was the new thing in town. But really, it just made sense to me that I would work at some type of fast food place near my house when I turned sixteen. I had been working since I was eight and ready to get my first real job.

At this donut shop, they sold mainly donuts and coffee. My favorite part was making the prohibited custom donuts, like double glazing the glazed donuts and mixing the custard and the jelly together for one plump sugar bomb. Once I really did eat a dozen donuts during break time. Of course, I did this when no one was looking.

My least favorite part was making coffee when everyone was looking.

After the training video, I made a huge mistake. It started with opening the bag of coffee for the giant coffee maker. Everything looked good to me as I loaded up coffee grounds into the basket. I lifted the basket back up to the top for the water to magically turn into coffee. In a short few minutes, I took a drive-through order, and the next thing everyone waiting in line saw was a cascade of coffee and grounds flowing from the open spout of the coffee machine.

Honestly, that was by far a better moment to capture for a training video. The waterfall of coffee and grounds mesmerized me until someone told me to turn the spout off. We all had to help clean up the mess, and then my manager, who cast me in the video, showed me the basket had no filter. After that, I secretly swore I would never drink coffee again.

As life went on, I stayed away from coffee. Oh, when traveling, I tried a cup or two here or there. But, when I went to Italy a few years ago and tried Italian coffee, I swore to my inner donut child it wasn't really coffee because it was Italian.

One day during July 2020, my acupuncturist said I could try coffee to give me more energy. I had been going to local coffee shops for takeout but only for tea, mainly for social interaction. But empowered with the recommendation, I decided to start with a cappuccino.

Instead of riding BART or the bus, I was using this money to try different cappuccinos…*cappuccini* at local coffee shops. It usually started on Mondays to help me kick off the week of job searching. Then I would get a cappuccino every time I had a job interview to give me that extra pep, or so I thought.

I liked talking to the cashiers and baristas – mostly small talk, of course. When outdoor seating opened, it was almost like sitting inside. When I used only to drink tea, pre-pandemic, I would sit for hours at a coffee shop near the Pistachio Palace and talk to the regulars and baristas. Now people are much more reserved and don't intermix with others as much. One day, I saw two huge dogs and watched as the owner said to someone else they were over six feet tall when standing. I felt too far away to jump in and say anything.

Some days when I look in the mirror now, after drinking coffee for almost a year, I wonder when my teeth will turn brown. And, I rarely drink wine these days, so I know whatever discoloration will surely come from all the coffee I've been drinking. But I'm over forty and know these things will happen. Just like when I asked a 27-year old to meet for a coffee after we connected on pandemic speed dating in February of 2021. He said yes, then he said no, giving the reason that I was too old.

But no one is too old to enjoy a coffee or the time spent sharing a coffee together.

6 Numbers Game

Whenever I take the Myers Briggs test, I come out an extrovert. But, I always take this test alone.

So, during the pandemic, I'd ask myself, if I'm an extrovert, why am I alone?

For the first time in my life, I felt that no matter if I was an extrovert or an introvert, I did not want to be alone. I've spent most of my life riding solo, but there were always people around, until lockdown.

And, while studying abroad in South America and working in Europe prepared me to handle unpredictable situations, like a bus catching fire, I never felt like I did during the pandemic. For a few months of lockdown in 2020, I had a set time of 5:00 pm to watch *The Golden Girls* but not to be reminded of my youth watching the show. I wanted the friendship that the girls had; they were never alone.

Then I just started signing up and signing up and signing up for virtual events – I mean, I went to like over 400 virtual events. And at one event, I met this guy, who I gave my number to, and he texted me,

"Why are you single?"

And, as my saying goes, "There are no stupid questions…that I have to answer."

The socially acceptable answer would have been, "It's a numbers game." This was first explained to me by my roommate's ex-boyfriend during a house party. It was right after 9/11, and I was living with a recently divorced woman in a two-bedroom Tudor house in Washington, D.C.

From parties to dinner guests, there was a lot of social activity at that house, and it was all her idea. For Halloween, it was her idea to have me dress up like her, which I did. She also influenced me to get my hair chemically straightened because she said I looked better with straight hair. So I did, and, for the record, I looked like a wet mouse until my curls came back.

Now, this ex-boyfriend of hers was a regular at these parties, sometimes with his new girlfriend. I distinctly remember asking what numbers were involved in this game. As I listened to him explain having a quota of men to date before Mr. Right would gallop in to be the winning number, it all sounded horrible.

I mean, a quota of men to meet? That didn't sound right to me.

I can't think of a book or movie where someone introduced themselves with a number or whispered in another's ear over a romantic dinner, "It's me. I am your number 17." And, when have you gotten a wedding invitation, "Announcing the marriage of his no. 55 and her no. 67?" You could possibly take an average for the wedding favors, since two are becoming one.

Maybe some people know what their quota is, but

I don't. I also don't want anyone to tell me either. I never think that the next man I meet will be my winning number.

I hadn't thought about the "numbers game" theory until the pandemic. With so much time on my hands, I thought I would give dating apps another try. So, I did hit my numbers regularly because I would run out of matches. I deleted my account shortly after meeting one man that only wanted to take pictures for my dating profile because he thought it would help me get more matches because he told me we weren't a match, even though the algorithm thought we were. And, I tried virtual speed dating, also hitting my numbers by getting no mutual matches and a guy that told me I was disqualified from even getting a coffee with him because I was too old.

From the bottom of my heart, I'm very happy I wasn't the right number for a guy I dated in San Francisco who told me he couldn't have any more relationships and that the next woman he dated, after me, would be the one he would marry because he was too tired of dating. I can say now, it would have been no fun to spend the pandemic with him, calculating only God knows what. Maybe he was psychic to know about his lucky number, or maybe he was one of the men they talk about in those articles that say men marry based on timing. Or maybe, some men just love timing and numbers more than romance.

Look, I am obviously not a quantitative woman. But for those of you that are doing the dating numbers game thing, just say, I'm looking for my better 50%. I mean, if people like numbers so much, just start speaking in numbers. For some, that is what +1 is all about anyway.

If the pandemic taught us anything, it was that time, and numbers can play tricks on us. But, according to Vedic astrology, our lives from birth are organized by chapters of years influenced by the planets. This isn't so much a numbers game but an ancient system that has predicted when I am 42, there is a chance that I could find my partner or my partner would find me. Somehow, they neglected to tell me anything about being alone during a pandemic leading up to meeting this partner.

While I could hit the partner jackpot this year, I continue to gamble without caring about my odds, still a believer in romance without numbers.

About the Author

L.B. Lewis is an American writer based in Los Angeles. She is the author of four books and her second novel, A MINOR DETOUR, rose to #12 on Amazon's New Adult Best Sellers in 2018. In 2021, SMALL TALK WITH MYSELF was a #1 Amazon New Release in Humor and Entertainment Short Reads. Visit: LBLewis.com.